THE POCKET GUIDE TO
NEURODIVERSITY

The
POCKET GUIDE
to
NEURODIVERSITY

Daniel Aherne
Illustrated by Tim Stringer

Jessica Kingsley Publishers
London and Philadelphia

First published in Great Britain in 2023 by Jessica Kingsley Publishers
An imprint of Hodder & Stoughton Ltd
An Hachette UK Company

1

The fonts, layout and overall design of this book have been prepared
according to dyslexia-friendly principles. At JKP we aim to make our
books' content accessible to as many readers as possible.

A CIP catalogue record for this title is available from the British
Library and the Library of Congress

ISBN 978 1 83997 014 6
eISBN 978 1 83997 015 3

Jessica Kingsley Publishers' policy is to use papers that are natural,
renewable and recyclable products and made from wood grown
in sustainable forests. The logging and manufacturing processes
are expected to conform to the environmental regulations
of the country of origin.

Jessica Kingsley Publishers
Carmelite House
50 Victoria Embankment
London EC4Y 0DZ

www.jkp.com

CONTENTS

	Acknowledgements	*8*
	Preface	*11*
Ch 1:	Neurodiversity Explained	**15**
Ch 2:	Neurotypes	**25**
Ch 3:	Processing	**51**
Ch 4:	Working Memory	**63**
Ch 5:	Communication	**70**
Ch 6:	Unwritten Rules	**82**
Ch 7:	Emotions	**90**
Ch 8:	Problem-Solving	**99**
	Conclusion	**106**
	Neurodiversity Resources	*109*
	References	*112*
	Index	*122*

This book is dedicated to those who cannot be saved by spellcheck.

ACKNOWLEDGEMENTS

I would like to thank three groups of people for making this book happen. First, the people who enabled the publication process. This started with Amy Lankester-Owen at Jessica Kingsley Publishers, who heard me speak and thought that my speech had the foundations for a book!

Following a neurodiversity talk I delivered to Hachette and Jessica Kingsley Publishers, Amy emailed me (perhaps the best email I have ever received!) and floated the idea of a pocket guide based on my talk. I said yes and then promptly did nothing. So, the next person I want to thank is Isabel Martin, who transcribed my talk and helped me to get all the words on paper.

Next came an editor and writer who I knew through my

work with my company, Adjust: the amazing Marianne Eloise, who helped me turn the transcription into a semblance of a book! And lastly, Lucy Cowie, who worked with me very patiently, sensitively and in such an understanding way, to produce the final version.

Maria Esteban and David Perkins, two of my managers when I worked at the National Autistic Society (NAS), are the second group of people I would like to thank.

Maria was my first manager when I worked at an NAS day centre in Croydon, and she helped me to understand that everything I had read about autism at university was pretty much wrong and useless! During the two years I worked with Maria, I learned so much about autism (plus a little Spanish!); lots of what Maria taught me has been the basis of my work for the last 15 years. Maria Esteban is an unsung hero, and she has done so much to enrich the lives of autistic people.

David Perkins was the manager of the NAS's employment service, Prospects, and I kept ringing him and asking for a job! Dave helped build my confidence and he let my entrepreneurial side shine. He was always on hand to give advice about autism and how employers needed to be doing more to change. Dave has become a great friend and mentor to me.

The last group I want to thank is the unbelievable neurodiversity community. I have learned so much from you all and I know that you will continue to educate and motivate me. There are too many inspiring individuals for me to be able to thank everyone personally, but my passion for neurodiversity first started when I volunteered with the autistic boy in 2000, grew by working with an amazing group of people at the National Autistic Society in 2005, and it continues to this day in my work.

Daniel Aherne, 2022

PREFACE

My name is Daniel Aherne, and this is my guide to the fascinating and hotly debated topic of neurodiversity. For more than 2o years I have been working with neurodivergent people, supporting them to thrive in a world that isn't always sensitive to their needs.

My company, Adjust,[1] provides training and consultancy to global businesses with the aim of helping them to better understand neurodivergent employees. We raise awareness of neurodiversity in the workplace in a clear, practical and positive way.

Our sessions include an introductory 'Lunch and Learn' to help companies learn about neurodiversity, training

---

1   www.adjustservices.co.uk/about

to ensure the recruitment process is as inclusive as possible and management training to ensure that managers can support and retain neurodivergent employees.

Adjust's mission, 'to start the neurodiversity conversation', is focused on the workplace, but I believe that there are huge benefits to this conversation taking place everywhere: in schools, communities, healthcare settings, offices and beyond.

My passion for raising the profile of neurodiversity also comes from personal experience. I was diagnosed with ADHD (attention deficit hyperactivity disorder) as an adult and, as a neurodivergent person myself, I genuinely understand how vital it is that we value the unique perspectives of neurodivergent people.

As I progressed through the UK education system in the late 1990s, which was largely exam-based, I experienced first-hand the challenges that neurodivergent students face in the school environment. Later, in the workplace, I noticed the barriers that stopped neurodivergent employees from getting into employment and excelling in their roles.

ONS (Office for National Statistics) data for 2021 shows that this trend continues today: they estimate that only 29 per cent of autistic people are in employment (ONS, 2021). Even before I received my own ADHD diagnosis, it was clear to me that some neurodivergent people were encountering major obstacles in their daily lives and that this needed to change.

As soon as careers started being discussed at school, I realized that I wanted to do a job that involved moving about; I knew I could never be office-based all week! I also thought that I could put my verbal skills, empathy and emotional intelligence to good use by supporting others.

So, at the age of 17, I decided I wanted to be a social worker, and after a social worker advised me to gain some volunteering experience, I started working on a playscheme, supporting an autistic boy. This experience, back in the year 2000, really lit a passion in me, and I never became a social worker! Instead, it kick-started my commitment to raising awareness of neurodiversity. I went on to work with autistic adults at the National Autistic Society (NAS), helping them to access employment and volunteering opportunities.

In this role, I started to notice the same barriers in workplaces arising again and again. Although every autistic person I was working with was different, almost every workplace had the same structural barriers. This made me realize the positive impact I could have by working with employers to make their businesses more inclusive.

As I researched neurodiversity, I learned that neurodivergent people like myself are not rare:

estimates suggest that at least 15 per cent of the UK population are neurodivergent (ACAS, n.d.). Neurodiversity is extremely common; some readers of this guide may be neurodivergent, most will have neurodivergent friends, relatives or colleagues.

Wherever there are people, there is a need to understand neurodiversity, and this guide aims to provide an introductory understanding of neurodiversity in an engaging and practical way. Everyday examples and the voices of neurodivergent people are included throughout; I hope these will spark your interest in neurodiversity.

By better understanding our neurodivergent colleagues, friends, neighbours and family members, we can create adaptable communities that work well for everyone.

CHAPTER 1

NEURODIVERSITY EXPLAINED

It is estimated that around one in seven adults are neurodivergent in some way (ACAS, n.d.), and while the complex diagnostic process makes it difficult to confirm whether this figure is accurate or high enough, it gives an insight into how much more common neurodiversity is than you might expect. Based on this estimate, it is highly likely that there are neurodivergent people in many classrooms, workplaces and homes around the world.

But despite the data showing the scale of neurodiversity, many people still don't understand the concept of neurodiversity, the different neurotypes and the many benefits of thinking differently.

> Neurodiversity is my superpower and I proudly navigate life by my own rules and routines. Most people can't even imagine the wonderful way I view the world.

Bev Shah, *founder of the think tank and advocacy group City Hive (personal communication, April 2022)*

WHAT IS NEURODIVERSITY?

Essentially, neurodiversity refers to the rich natural diversity of human minds. To me, neurodiversity is the celebration, recognition and acceptance that we all experience the world in different ways.

The concept of neurodiversity was first conceived by a sociologist called Judy Singer in 1998, and it was revolutionary at a time when people saw neurodivergent conditions as a burden or hindrance to the individual and those around them (Singer, n.d.). The term first appeared in print in 1998, when the journalist Harvey Blume compared neurodiversity to biodiversity: 'Neurodiversity may be every bit as crucial for the human race as biodiversity is for life in general' (Blume, 1998).

Singer believed that all brains are different, and that we all think and process the world in a different way. She is the author of *NeuroDiversity: The Birth of an Idea*.

As the concept of neurodiversity has evolved, many workplaces and educational settings have adopted it as an umbrella term for various under-represented neurotypes and profiles.

NURTURING NEURODIVERSITY

In my training workshops I love to use the analogy of biodiversity, and I try to get everyone to think about a cactus. For example, a cactus flowers and blooms in the desert. Here, it thrives and really reaches its potential, but if we move that cactus from a desert in Arizona and plant it in my back garden in the UK, it might not thrive or survive. The climate would not be right for it.

However, we would never say that the cactus is broken, or that there's a deficit with this cactus, or think that the cactus needs fixing or curing. We would realize that the environment wasn't right for the cactus to meet its potential. And we would recognize that for the cactus to fulfil its potential we may have to make adaptations to its environment; for the cactus to thrive in the UK, moving it into a greenhouse would better meet its needs for light and heat.

What if we thought about people's minds in this way, and we didn't say that someone who was struggling at school or work had a deficit or was broken? What if, instead, we considered how we could change the

environment for this person? As a society, what can we change to ensure that all individuals can thrive and reach their potential?

In my professional and personal experience, one of the biggest things we can do to improve someone's environment is to provide education and awareness to those around them. Greater empathy for and awareness of other people's differences can radically improve their day-to-day experiences. This philosophy is what motivates me to educate people about neurodiversity. And it's why I've written this guide.

NEURODIVERGENT IDENTITIES

A person is considered 'neurodivergent' if their brain works differently from the majority of people's brains. These differences may be apparent in neurodivergent people's learning styles, the way they are misunderstood and misjudged by others, and in their communication and processing.

Common neurodivergent identities include autism, dyslexia, dyspraxia (DCD), ADHD, Tourette's syndrome, dysgraphia and dyscalculia. There are lots of diagnostic overlaps between different neurotypes, and it is becoming increasingly common for people to identify with two or more of the neurotypes.

In this guide, I will focus on explaining more about autism, dyslexia, dyspraxia and ADHD; by understanding these four neurotypes a little better, you will be well on your way to becoming more neuro-inclusive. I hope that this awareness will lead you to think again about people's learning styles and communication preferences, as well as people you may have misunderstood or misjudged.

Neurodiversity might explain why your colleague struggles to make eye contact, your friend always interrupts you when you're speaking or your child is overwhelmed by loud noises.

Just like neurotypical people, neurodivergent people are all different. Neurodivergent people may have areas in which they excel and other areas that they struggle with: aspects of their functioning that might hold them back in a neurotypically designed world. While neurodivergent people will have different support needs, many of the barriers they may struggle with are societal or cultural, such as rigid schooling, communication differences or sensory challenges.

These barriers aren't the fault of the individual – neurodivergent people are simply navigating a world that was not set up with their needs in mind. By better understanding and even celebrating the many benefits of the different ways people think and communicate, we can make life easier for everyone.

I will never stop being neurodivergent, it is for life. But I actually love looking at the world through my eyes – it is a rainbow-coloured kaleidoscope. It keeps me active, gives me purpose and I feel I am changing the world every time I have a new idea!

Shofa Miah, *founder of the youth mental health charity Ashok's Vision: @ashoksvision (Miah, 2021)*

Many people have particular areas of interest that engage them more easily than others, but if they have a relatively typical neurological profile, it is unlikely that there will be a huge disparity in their skill set. They are less likely to be extraordinarily good at specific things whilst needing adjustments and support in others.

This neurotype is often described as 'neurotypical'. The majority of the population has this neurotype, and our society has developed in line with the needs of neurotypical people. A lot of neurodivergent people are discriminated against because we expect most people to fit into the neurotypically designed world.

For example, a neurotypical child may perform fairly consistently across a range of subjects, while a neurodivergent child might be perceived as having erratic results. Teachers and parents might find it hard to understand how a neurodivergent child can perform exceptionally well in some subjects but really struggle with others. They may have As in some subjects and Fs in others.

A neurodivergent person in the workplace may also have contrasting abilities, with noticeable areas of strengths alongside a need for adjustments in other areas that they may find more challenging. They may excel in some areas like problem-solving but need adjustments around things such as processing and organization.

Ensuring that every single person has the support they need, and that we understand difference, will mean that people can pursue the things they are best at and thrive, reaching their potential just like the cactus in the desert in Arizona.[1]

As awareness grows of the value of the skills neurodivergent people can possess, employers are realizing the benefits of recruiting people who think differently. For example, in the UK, the thinking skills of dyslexic people have been described as 'mission critical' for national security by the intelligence agency GCHQ (2021).

To understand neurodiversity is to understand that a range of neurotypes exist and to understand that many people communicate and experience the world differently from the majority. Collectively, we need to

---

[1] For more information on legal adjustments and how to access advice, see: www.gov.uk/reasonable-adjustments-for-disabled-workers

recognize and support the reality that some people need adjustments in workplace, educational or social settings to fulfil their potential. Maybe some individuals would thrive in an environment entirely different to the one they struggle in or would be more at ease in an environment with more flexible rules.

What we can all do is identify areas where we can offer that flexibility and compassion. The aim of this book is to give you a brief introduction to neurodiversity and develop your understanding of this concept. I hope that reading it inspires you to think beyond the idea of differences as deficits and to celebrate the benefits of thinking differently!

ψ KEY TAKEAWAYS

- Neurodiversity refers to the rich natural diversity in human minds.

- Neurodivergence encompasses neurotypes such as autism, ADHD, dyslexia, dyspraxia and many more.

- One in seven people are estimated to be neurodivergent in some way.

- Neurodivergent people have unique strengths and challenges and can thrive in environments that support their needs.

ψ REFLECTION POINTS

- Does having more awareness of neurodiversity make you reflect on times when you may have misjudged someone or misunderstood their actions? How could you react differently in the future?

- What kind of adaptations might benefit the neurodivergent thinkers in your life?

CHAPTER 2

NEUROTYPES

Throughout my career, I've noticed a recurring theme, which is that many neurotypes, including those we focus on in this guide, overlap. This is shown by the intersecting diagnostic criteria for several neurodivergent profiles.

At the National Autistic Society, I discovered that a lot of autistic people I worked with also had ADHD, while others also had dyspraxia or dyslexia. Certain forms of behaviour overlap across neurotypes too; for example, some autistic people and people with ADHD may hyper-focus on interests or work that they find particularly interesting. And some autistic people, as well as people with dyslexia, dyspraxia and ADHD, can be incredibly creative.

Learning more about different neurodivergent identities or neurotypes can help us to support people's individual needs and to create conditions in which they can thrive. However, it is important to realize that we don't all necessarily fit into neat diagnostic boxes, and while diagnoses can often be constructive, everybody is unique and has different skills and challenges.

Not everyone with a neurodivergent thinking style is diagnosed. You may have children with a neurodivergent profile, but you might not know it yet. You may be neurodivergent yourself, but you have not needed to or been able to access a diagnosis. Barriers to diagnosis and therefore adjustments and understanding can mean people do not get to meet their true potential, and everyone deserves to have the support they need, regardless of formal diagnosis.

Perhaps one day, if we manage to create more neuro-inclusive societies, people will naturally think: 'What can I change about this person's environment to ensure that they can reach their potential?' However, at this stage of the journey towards understanding neurodiversity, it is necessary to be aware that different neurotypes exist and to learn about how they are defined.

CELEBRATING INDIVIDUALITY

John Elder Robinson, the autistic author of *Look Me in the Eye* (2009), explains that neurodiversity is the idea that neurological differences like autism and ADHD are the result of normal variation in the human genome. He introduces the concept that these neurotypes are a natural part of the human race. As a species, we need people who think differently and act differently so we can survive and thrive. If humans all thought in the same way, we would not have made such significant strides in our social, cultural and scientific development.

In this chapter, I want to offer a brief overview of four neurotypes – dyslexia, autism, ADHD and dyspraxia – bearing the overlaps between different neurodivergent identities in mind.

DYSLEXIA

Dyslexia is the most commonly diagnosed of the four neurotypes that this book focuses on. It has been estimated by the British Dyslexia Association that 10 per cent of the UK population has a dyslexia diagnosis (BDA, 2022; dyslexia.uk.com, 2022). To bring that figure to life, let's think about the UK population.

The UK population is currently estimated to be 70 million. So, 10 per cent of the UK population is seven million. Seven million people is more than three-quarters of the population of London. Imagine if most people in London had dyslexia! The majority of Londoners taking the Tube, catching buses and walking around shopping or going to work! Dyslexia isn't just something one person you knew at school had – it's far more common than you think.

Returning to the idea of overlapping diagnoses: up to 35 per cent of people with dyslexia have ADHD too. Neurodivergence rarely fits into neat little boxes, and diagnoses often overlap (Olivardia, 2020).

Even for individuals who only experience one neurodivergent condition, there can be many misconceptions about their experience of this condition. For example, we often associate dyslexia primarily with difficulty spelling, but that is only one part of dyslexia. Dyslexic people often have great visual skills and creativity, but we put them at a disadvantage in our current education system when we ask them to prove their understanding through reading, writing and written recall.

In her book *The Adult Side of Dyslexia* (2021), Kelli Sandman-Hurley interviews a series of dyslexic adults about their experiences. One interviewee describes how the set-up of the conventional school system and not having access to the right support caused her to experience low self-worth: 'I always viewed myself as the stupid slow kid who just couldn't read or spell. I had minimal self-worth from an academic perspective, which quickly spilled over into the personal areas of my life' (Sandman-Hurley, 2021, p.32).

By only offering limited metrics to measure ability, we overlook the many things dyslexic people can be exceptional at. This can leave dyslexic people with damaging self-esteem issues, which might not arise if we offered other metrics by which to measure their skills. Dyslexic people have always existed, long before formal education – how would we view dyslexia without those goalposts?

Like the cactus in Chapter 1 that can't thrive in the back gardens of Britain, a lot of dyslexic people can't fulfil their potential within the constraints of mainstream education. However, many dyslexic people are very empathetic, very intuitive and very good at visual thinking. They can be skilled at connecting the dots and pattern recognition, and are often highly inventive, creative and entrepreneurial.

When a dyslexic person is encouraged to pursue their skills rather than their difficulties, they can thrive. Dyslexic people will often excel in an environment that plays to their strengths, and with the right support they can be successful in any role!

Proudly dyslexic celebrities

A quick google of famous people with dyslexia will reveal a long list of celebrities who have been successful in a wide range of industries. Celebrities who have been vocal about their dyslexia as an asset include Jo Malone, Whoopi Goldberg and Richard Branson.

Jo Malone, who is famous for creating luxury fragrances, struggled in school because of the way that her intelligence and ability was measured. But when she left school, she became a very successful entrepreneur. As Jo Malone's success demonstrates, original thinking and creativity can be powerful skills in business.

Confronting challenges and stigma

Like the other three neurotypes explored in this guide, dyslexia can be stigmatized. Many dyslexic people do not receive a diagnosis until adulthood, especially if they have attended schools without the resources to diagnose dyslexia, and they may have lived for decades without support that could have helped them to thrive.

An important point to address about dyslexia is that about half of dyslexic people see words and sentences moving around when they read. A common misconception of dyslexia is that all dyslexic people see words as blurry. Or that words being blurry or moving around is only something that affects people with dyslexia. However, many other people with neurotypes such as autism and ADHD also experience this. This is called visual stress or Irlen syndrome, and be worse when someone is tired or stressed (Irlen, n.d.).

Before reading this passage, perhaps you thought this was all dyslexia was. But the experience of seeing moving text, or of having difficulties with writing or spelling, is just the tip of the iceberg for some dyslexic people, concealing many skills that lie beneath.

One of the major factors that contributes to a difficulty with reading for dyslexic people is white background and black writing. If you think about most educational resources, they feature black writing on a white background; this can have a disabling impact on people with a dyslexic profile. In your documents, try to avoid using black writing on a bright white background. In my training sessions, I choose to use an off-grey background on my slides; you can easily make changes like this in PowerPoint and Word.

Helpful adaptations

If dyslexia were to be better understood and supported in workplaces and educational settings, dyslexic people would be given access to things that enable them to work and learn more effectively.

Helpful adaptations include allowing increased time to process information; using yellow paper or softer-coloured PowerPoint slides instead of white; providing a computer in exams or providing speech-to-text software; and the option to present work visually or verbally rather than in writing. Awareness of the adjustments that can help dyslexic people on a day-to-day basis can enable them to reach their full potential.

AUTISM

Autism is a neurotype that affects the way someone experiences the world and communicates with other people. It exists on a spectrum, and there can be significant variation in the strengths and challenges that different autistic people have; for example, some autistic people are able to work full-time without needing any workplace adjustments, some require minimal adjustments such as a fixed desk, while others have learning disabilities and need support on a daily basis.

Autistic people can often be incredibly passionate and

throw themselves completely into anything they're excited by or interested in.

Barriers for autistic people may include the sensory environment of a school, a shop or a workplace. Verbal communication can also be an area of difficulty when communicating with neurotypical colleagues or peers, and individuals might struggle to maintain eye contact, pick up on jokes and/or sarcasm, or gauge what another person is feeling through their facial expression or tone of voice. However, studies have shown that autistic people often thrive when communicating with each other (Crompton, Ropar, Evans-Williams, et al., 2020).

Damian Milton's (2018) research on the 'double empathy problem' suggests that while autistic people often communicate well with each other, neurotypical people can sometimes misunderstand or not communicate clearly with autistic people. The expectations and cultural differences of neurotypical communication can create a barrier.

Challenges with understanding unwritten rules in schools, social settings or workplaces can also cause difficulties for autistic people.

The language debate
There are many different labels for autism and autistic people (these include: 'autistic person', 'person with

autism', 'person on the spectrum', 'Asperger's',[1] 'Aspie'
and 'autism spectrum disorder' or 'ASD'). For clarity, I
will use 'autism' or 'autistic' through this guide, as that's
the language many autistic adults and advocates use for
themselves.

Identity-first language (for example, saying 'autistic
person' or 'I am autistic', rather than 'person with
autism') is preferred by many autistic individuals
because it recognizes that autism is an inherent part
of a person's identity, and one which impacts many
other areas of their experience (Brown, 2022). It is not
something to be cured or overcome, and in placing that
linguistic emphasis on autism as an identity, advocates
argue that you emphasize the inherent value of autistic
individuals.

Back in the year 2000, when I first learned about autism,
I was encouraged by non-autistic people to use the
'person-first' phrase 'people with autism'. However,

---

1   Asperger syndrome is not included in the *Diagnostic and
    Statistical Manual of Mental Disorders*, 5th Edition, and so
    many people who would have previously fit this profile are now
    diagnosed with autism spectrum disorder (ASD) instead. Some
    individuals who did receive a diagnosis of Asperger syndrome
    may prefer to continue using the term, whilst others refer to
    themselves as autistic or as being on the autism spectrum.

    For more information, see: www.autism.org.uk/advice-and-
    guidance/what-is-autism/asperger-syndrome or
    www.spectrumnews.org/opinion/viewpoint/why-fold-asperger-
    syndrome-into-autism-spectrum-disorder-in-the-dsm-5

over the past two decades, as autistic advocacy has grown stronger, I have listened to the views of many autistic people and I now understand that person-first language is not the preference for the majority of the autistic community. But it is always important to respect personal preferences about language and to respect every autistic person as a unique individual.

Early in my career I asked an autistic person, Ross, which label he preferred. His reply was 'Ross'. This was a great reminder that there is always an individual in front of you! If you are not autistic and you are speaking to and/or working with an autistic person, always use their preferred terminology.

Prevalence and diagnosis

It has been estimated by the National Autistic Society (NAS) that 1.1 per cent of the UK population is autistic (NAS, 2o22c), but the true figure is almost certainly higher, partly because many people do not get diagnosed.

White men or boys represent the majority of people who receive an autism diagnosis. However, in recent years there has been a push to redress the diagnostic balance in relation to gender and ethnicity. At the time of writing, the male-to-female ratio of diagnosis is three to one (Loomes, Hull and Mandy, 2o17; NAS, 2o22a), but there is a growing awareness that girls and women may be under-diagnosed.

Women and girls are often diagnosed late because they present differently and often 'mask' their difficulties more than men and boys. Masking, or camouflaging, is a self-protecting mechanism wherein someone will imitate others or hide their true self and behaviours to fit in. However, over time, this can cause burnout and meltdowns, and seriously damage mental health.

I've worked with girls who receive many other diagnoses, such as borderline personality disorder, eating disorders, anxiety and ODD (oppositional defiant disorder), before they get an autism diagnosis, which means they go without the specific understanding and support they need. On the other hand, boys are often diagnosed much earlier and autism is frequently their first diagnosis.

It is important to note that access to diagnosis for all groups is a real barrier; there are many different autistic expressions, and many boys and men may also mask. It is also vital to recognize the many different gender identities that exist and to consider the different presentations of autism across these (NAS, 2022b).

Myths, misconceptions and stereotypes

There are a lot of misconceptions and myths around autism. For instance, you may be aware of the myth that the measles, mumps and rubella (MMR) jab caused autism. This has been completely disproved (CDC, 2022; Taylor, Miller and Farrington et al., 1999) and is very unhelpful to the autistic community. I recently heard the phrase, 'Vaccines don't cause autism. Autism causes vaccines,' which refers to the fact that many people in the scientific community might be autistic, and that these gifted scientists are the people who come up with life-saving vaccines. I love that idea.

This topic brings me on to the issue of stereotyping that I often discuss in my workshops. Many scientists and inventors in the past may have been autistic. Today, high-profile autistic people in science and technology include biochemist and prize-winning author Dr Camilla Pang (2019), and the entrepreneur and engineer Elon Musk (SNL, 2021).

However, despite much evidence of autistic people successfully applying their creativity to technological innovation, scientific problem-solving and artistic expression, there is still a common myth that autistic people can't be creative. This may have been compounded by the 'triad of impairments' medical model of autism that views autistic people as having a lack of 'social imagination'.

The triad of impairments said autistic people had a deficit in three main areas: social imagination, social communication and social interaction. But this theory is challenged by the many autistic people who thrive in creative fields such as fine art, theatre, literature, music and dance.

Proudly autistic celebrities

Anthony Hopkins and Daryl Hannah are autistic actors who have described how being autistic has helped them to become successful in film and theatre (Willingham, 2013; Gannon, 2017). Many autistic people have expansive imaginations, and I have often speculated that this may be due to not being constrained by conventional neurotypical thinking and to being able to imagine things that other people have simply never thought of!

Dan Aykroyd of *Ghostbusters* fame is also autistic (Strombo, 2013), and recently British celebrities such as Christine McGuinness (Barnfield, 2021) and Chris Packham have openly discussed being autistic:

> **Humanity has prospered because of people with autistic traits. Without them, we wouldn't have put man on the Moon or be running software programs.**
>
> ***Chris Packham,*** *presenter, photographer and author (Battersby, 2018)*

Helpful adaptations

Autistic people often struggle with change, so I often suggest adjustments to accommodate for this. For example, in workshops, I advise managers that we can ensure autistic people reach their potential by communicating information about changes in advance or by reducing change as much as possible, thereby reducing uncertainty.

For instance, in workplace settings, I have helped people to receive adjustments around change. One autistic man I supported, who was employed by a large department store, only worked on a specific till in menswear. Other constructive adaptations I have suggested include giving autistic employees their own parking space, or allowing them to be exempt from hot-desking policies; the uncertainty of not knowing where to park or to sit at work can cause intense anxiety.

Adjustments that may be beneficial to autistic people both within and beyond the workplace include warning them in advance about changes in routine; repeating or clarifying expressions if needed; allowing extra time for processing information; and not placing significant expectations on communication, for example, understanding that it is not rude if an individual doesn't make eye contact.

ADHD

Many people with ADHD describe it as being both one of the 'best' and 'worst' parts of their identity. Discussing his experiences of having ADHD, musician Loyle Carner says, 'It is the best and worst thing about me. You know, I love it but I hate it. But me being ADHD, it's just who I am. All the best things about me come from it – being emotionally intelligent, being passionate, being inquisitive' (Levine, 2019).

When you think of ADHD, you're likely to think of naughty boys playing up in the classroom, but it's much more complicated. This assumption can be damaging too: women and people of colour sometimes face barriers to diagnosis due to the stereotype of a person with ADHD typically being a child who is white. In my work I have met a diverse range of people with ADHD who are very charismatic, sensitive, passionate, creative and outcome-focused, and who have unique ways of solving problems.

Prevalence and characteristics

The prevalence of ADHD within the population is estimated to be approximately 5 per cent (ADHD UK, n.d.). There is some variation in ADHD prevalence between children and adults, with lower rates of diagnosis documented among adults, but this may reflect changes in environment and expectations at different stages of development. Despite the persistent stereotype that ADHD only affects children (diagnostic tests for adults in the UK were only introduced relatively recently), it is a life-long profile.

ADHD is defined by inattention, hyperactivity and impulsivity, and a person might have it without the hyperactive element, which can make it harder for them to get diagnosed, particularly for girls.

ADHD is characterized by many different behaviours, including an inability to sit still, excessive physical movement, impulsivity, an inability to wait to take turns and an inability to concentrate.

While poor concentration is one diagnostic symptom, it doesn't solely define ADHD – in some ways, it can be too much concentration on the 'wrong' thing in strict school environments that can get people in trouble! For example, a person who is passionate about *Star Wars* might be able to focus for hours on learning everything about that universe but would struggle to concentrate when faced with routine school tasks.

However, this ability to intensely focus can be advantageous in some settings, particularly when someone works with their preferred topics or interests. The greatest swimmer of all time, Michael Phelps, has ADHD. When he was young, his mum noticed that her son struggled to concentrate on maths, so she hired a tutor and encouraged the tutor to adapt questions to relate to Michael's passion for swimming: 'How long would it take to swim 500 meters if you swim three meters per second?' (Dutton, 2021).

Michael Phelps's mother's realization that her son had the potential to focus exceptionally well when he was engaged may have helped to enable his sporting success. If Michael Phelps had only ever encountered environments that didn't support his way of thinking or working, he may not have been as successful.

Hyper-focus

Michael Phelps is one of many sports stars who have ADHD; other high-performing sports professionals with ADHD include Simone Biles (Rodden, 2021) and Michael Jordan (Archer, 2014). It could be argued that there is an overlap between ADHD and a proficiency for the laser focus, dedication and energy that many sports require.

Another thing that can really help with hyper-focus is pressure. Like many people with ADHD, if I have a deadline I will do the work just before the deadline, as the pressure and urgency help me to focus most effectively and that's when I get stuff done. A fast-paced career such as working in sport can suit many individuals with ADHD, while jobs in which you work to very clear deadlines, such as journalism, can also be a good professional fit for people with ADHD.

When I worked in a medical school, lots of the paramedics had ADHD, and the high-pressure conditions of their working environment suited them. The hyper-focus that they had when they went to an incident combined with their super-fast processing meant they were very good at their jobs.

I was working with paramedics because I was a

disability advisor at a university, and the paramedics had been forced off the field to do written work for what was referred to as CPD (continuing professional development). Think back to that biodiversity analogy: in a formal academic environment poorly suited to their needs, the paramedics became disabled. But when they were out in the field they thrived, just like the cactus in the desert in Arizona.

Celebrities with ADHD

The hyper-focus, dedication and high energy associated with ADHD can lead to success in many fields beyond sports too. Several famous musicians and actors, including Mel B (Ojomu, 2019), Zooey Deschanel (Freeth, 2021) and Justin Timberlake (Weintraub, 2008), have spoken publicly about their perceptions of both the benefits and challenges of having ADHD.

Comedian Rory Bremner has described his life with ADHD as 'a bit like plate spinning sometimes, I feel like my life used to be like how you see circus acts with six plates spinning and there's always one just about to fall off – sometimes your life can be like that' (Bedigan, 2022).

Helpful adaptations

There are a number of straightforward adaptations that can enable people with ADHD to thrive rather than struggle in workplaces, classrooms and social settings. Accepting and promoting the need for frequent movement can help to reduce restlessness and aid concentration, while standing desks, walking meetings and outdoor learning can also enhance focus.

DYSPRAXIA

It is estimated by the Dyspraxia Association that 3–5 per cent of the population has dyspraxia, also known as 'developmental coordination disorder' (*BBC Yorkshire*, 2021).

While developmental coordination disorder, or DCD, is the official diagnostic term, the term dyspraxia is commonly used. In this guide, I will use the term dyspraxia. The neurodiversity movement focuses on recognizing the positive aspects of under-represented neurotypes whilst still addressing the barriers that can exist for people. So where possible I will avoid using the term 'disorder'. This change in language is vital, as the impact of negative terms can affect people's self-esteem and confidence.

Coordination and planning

Dyspraxia is commonly associated with difficulties with coordination. This is often broken down into 'gross motor skills' (such as catching a ball or riding a bike), fine motor skills (such as writing or doing up shoelaces) and balance. This can create challenges with things such as handwriting or learning to drive a car, and dyspraxic individuals might take longer to learn new skills requiring coordination.

Dyspraxia is also associated with difficulties with planning and organization, which is where there is an overlap with dyslexia or ADHD. I often compare dyspraxia to having all the jigsaw pieces in your mind but no jigsaw-box picture to copy. It can also affect sense of direction, meaning that dyspraxic people often get lost. I have a diagnosis of ADHD but I identify strongly with the strengths and challenges of dyspraxia too, including struggling with my sense of direction; a lot of the time I just get a cab to avoid getting lost!

To give you a more vivid idea of the prevalence of dyspraxia: if we think of about 5 per cent of the UK population having dyspraxia, that's roughly equivalent to the size of the population of Wales. If everyone in Wales had dyspraxia, we would know much more about it. Dyspraxia often seems to be the least well known of all the neurodivergent profiles. You might think a dyspraxic person is simply clumsy, but it's more complex than that.

Proudly dyspraxic celebrities
The dyspraxic actor Daniel Radcliffe once joked, 'I sometimes think, "Why, oh why, hasn't Velcro taken

off?"', because he finds it hard to tie his shoelaces up (Tobin, 2008; *Evening Standard*, 2008). However, despite the challenges Radcliffe has experienced with clothing, he has spent his successful acting career using his communication and creativity skills. Many people that I have met with dyspraxia often demonstrate real creative flair and strong emotional intelligence.

I think it is vital to redress the unbalanced perception many people have of dyspraxia and to focus on some of the positive aspects. Radcliffe struggled with his coordination and has said that he found school difficult, but in film he found an industry he could thrive in.

Florence Welch, the singer in the band Florence and the Machine, is also dyspraxic, and she is best known for making music and dancing – challenging the simplicity of the 'clumsy' stereotype (Holland, 2012). There is always more to the lived experiences of people than you realize at first, and while dyspraxia affects your coordination, it doesn't mean you can't achieve, even in quite physical areas. In fact, the English rugby union player Ellis Genge is dyspraxic, and he has spoken openly about his dyspraxia in the past (Mead, 2021).

As always, people might have incredible abilities in some areas due to their neurotype, but in others they might need adjustments. These adjustments could be as simple as being patient and understanding when you perceive someone to be flaky or clumsy: there could be more to it!

Helpful adaptations

People with dyspraxia may struggle with aspects of dressing – for example, doing up buttons or tying shoelaces – but these challenges don't mean that they are slapdash or careless. Due to difficulties with directions, dyspraxic people may also find it harder than many neurotypical people to arrive at a new place on time. Greater tolerance and flexibility around appearance and punctuality may help dyspraxic people to feel more comfortable.

Ψ KEY TAKEAWAYS

- There can often be overlaps between different neurodivergent identities.

- Not everyone with a neurodivergent condition is diagnosed, and many people may be neurodivergent without knowing it. Regardless of formal diagnosis, everyone deserves the support they need.

- Dyslexia is the most commonly diagnosed neurodivergent condition: an estimated one in ten people have a dyslexia diagnosis.

- Dyslexic people are often very creative and entrepreneurial, with great visual skills, but are put at a disadvantage by our formal education system's focus on reading, writing and spelling.

- Adjustments that can help support dyslexic people include extra processing time, text-to-speech or speech-to-text software, using a keyboard rather than pen and paper, and using soft-coloured paper or screen backgrounds when reading.

- Celebrities who have spoken openly about being dyslexic include Whoopi Goldberg and Jo Malone.

- Autism impacts the way an individual communicates and experiences the world.

- Common autistic traits include communication differences, intense topics of interest, sensory processing difficulties, difficulty interpreting jokes and/or sarcasm and in maintaining eye contact.

- Autism has many labels; these include 'autistic', 'autism spectrum', 'Aspie' and more. It is important to respect an autistic individual's preferred terminology when referring to their condition.

- Many autistic people 'mask' their autistic characteristics as a defence mechanism, which can eventually lead to burnout or meltdowns.

- Masking is more common in autistic women and girls, which can result in late diagnosis.

- Autistic people can be supported with adjustments including reducing uncertainty where possible, and allowing for routine and consistency, such as giving an individual the same parking spot or place to work.

- ADHD is defined by inattention, hyperactivity and impulsivity, but can exist without the hyperactive element (sometimes referred to as ADD).

- It is characterized by behaviours including impulsivity, an inability to wait or sit still and difficulty concentrating.

- People with ADHD can often thrive in fast-paced careers including sports and journalism, but can succeed in any field with the right adjustments.

- It is estimated that 3–5 per cent of the UK population has dyspraxia.

- Dyspraxia is associated with difficulties with coordination, balance, and gross and fine motor skills, but it can also cause issues with working memory and concentration.

ψ REFLECTION POINTS

- Can we make it easier for people to express their knowledge and understanding in different ways? Some dyslexic people can articulate their understanding amazingly well in speech.

- Many dyslexic people are creative and original thinkers. What benefits can this have for society?

- Why do you think masking might be so emotionally draining for an autistic person? Do you think masking would be less common in a more inclusive society?

- How could your workplace, school or community adapt to better meet the needs of autistic people?

- Could you introduce more movement into your social or professional interactions?

- Have you misjudged people in the past by assuming they may not be listening to you because they are fidgeting or interrupt you? Does understanding more about ADHD make you reconsider your previous assumptions?

- What was your initial understanding of dyspraxia? Has reading this chapter changed your perception?

CHAPTER 3

PROCESSING

Differences in cognitive and sensory processing are common among neurodivergent people. Some neurodivergent people may find it challenging to process information as quickly as other people might expect them to, while sensory processing difficulties can mean that neurodivergent individuals struggle with certain sounds, tastes, textures, bright lights and busy environments.

Issues with sensory processing can also influence and complicate how a neurodivergent person experiences cognitive processing. For example, if an autistic person is in a noisy and busy crowded place and becomes overwhelmed, it can make it more difficult for them to process thoughts and information, potentially leading to meltdown.

REFLECTIVE PROCESSING

I often say that neurodivergent people are the only people who fully listen to what I say, because many of them really take time to understand what I am saying!

I worked with an autistic man who had been referred to the National Autistic Society by his local job centre to access support to get a job. They told me that he was completely non-verbal and did not speak, but after I had worked with him for a few weeks, I found that he could speak. He just needed longer than you might anticipate to reflectively process what you had said, and he needed to be asked one question at a time.

People would often ask him, 'How are you? How did you get here today?' That's two questions to process. His processing time was around 15 seconds, so if I just asked, 'How are you?' and waited 15 seconds for a reply, he was able to respond. Little adjustments such as this can make life so much easier for people who have a different way of listening and processing.

That is the most extreme version of reflective processing I've ever come across. I usually find that, for a lot of dyslexic people, processing might take three to four seconds, or perhaps a bit longer when they're reading. I often say, 'If the computer page takes longer to load, it doesn't mean it contains any less important information.' Frequently it means there's more information being accessed.

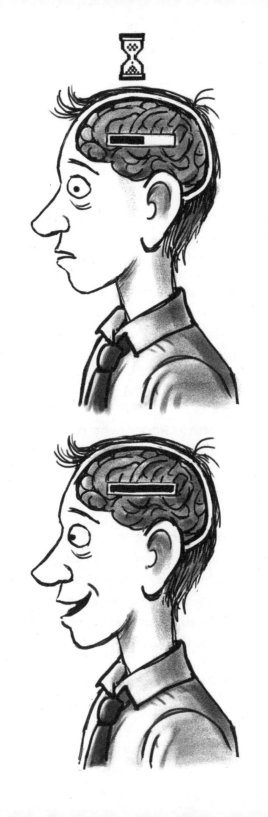

We all operate at different speeds and as the author and advocate of the slow movement Carl Honoré explains, 'everyone has their own personal metronome' (Magidoff, 2021).

I don't want to look at processing in a negative way, but it is a difference for some neurodivergent people. Greater tolerance of reflective processing could be constructive for us all.

In many circumstances, whether at school, at work or in a social setting, someone with reflective processing may have been labelled as 'slow'. I don't agree with that negative terminology. It simply means that someone takes longer to absorb information, process it and formulate a response.

Author Maxine Frances Roper, who has ADHD and dyspraxia, describes how her processing speed as a child has affected her communication as an adult:

I tend to open up to people quickly and am known as a good listener. I'm proud of these things, but I think they're partly ways I overcompensate for being misread as shy or disengaged because I process certain things more slowly, particularly when I was younger.

Maxine Frances Roper, *author with dyspraxia and ADHD (personal communication, November 2021)*

SUPER-FAST PROCESSING

In contrast, I've worked with a lot of people with ADHD who have super-fast processing and seem to know what you're going to say before you say it, and even answer your question before you've asked it. As a consequence, people with super-fast processing can be perceived as rude because they cut people off before they've finished speaking.

Super-fast processing can be a positive and people can come across as charismatic, witty, sharp, and able to grasp concepts and see the bigger picture quickly.

People with any neurodivergent condition may struggle with processing in different ways, and it's important to ask an individual which adjustments can be put in place to help them.

SENSORY PROCESSING

The sensory differences that many neurodivergent people have are often referred to as 'sensory processing difficulties', in which the brain has difficulty receiving and responding to information that comes through the senses. This might manifest as a neurodivergent person being unable to filter out certain sounds, being able to smell too much, finding certain textures painful or even being clumsy.

We most often associate sensory issues with autistic people, some of whom can even hear electricity in the walls or might find loud noises painful. Certain aspects of sensory processing can be difficult to experience, and misconceptions around how sensory processing is experienced can make life complicated for neurodivergent people.

For example, if a person struggles in a classroom or social setting because they find it too noisy or overstimulating, it can make it very hard to function. Sensory overwhelm might cause a meltdown or other distress, which to an outside observer might look like a 'tantrum'.

Better understanding of the fact that someone who is experiencing sensory overload is in genuine distress would relieve a lot of stress for people with sensory processing issues, but there are also other ways that the risk can be mitigated.

For example, someone might benefit from wearing earplugs in loud places, or spending time alone if they feel overloaded. They may also prefer to remove labels from clothes or only wear certain materials against their skin. Forcing somebody to 'get used' to something that they find painful or distressing can be very traumatic.

In her book *The Spectrum Girl's Survival Guide*, Siena Castellon writes:

> Having sensory sensitivities is a large part of being autistic. Not being able to filter out sensory information can be intolerable, especially at the end of a long day when our defences have been weakened. Yet since most neurotypical people don't experience sensory overloads, they cannot fully understand how distressing, overwhelming and painful they can be[...] Trying to build up sensory tolerance and ignoring sensory sensitivities does not work.

Siena Castellon, *author (Castellon, 2020, pp.58–60)*

Heightened sensory sensitivity

A lot of neurodivergent people have heightened sensory sensitivity, and that might be to touch, smell, taste, light or a combination of all of these. Sometimes this can be quite disabling, but sometimes it can be quite enabling in the right circumstances or environment – providing a distinct lens that a neurodivergent person views and experiences the world through.

As mentioned earlier, Jo Malone, the perfumer, is dyslexic. At school she struggled greatly and was considered 'severely' impaired in a setting where intelligence was solely measured through written words (*BBC News*, 2015). She left school at the age of 13 to care for her mother, and in some circumstances might have struggled to get through life.

Like many neurodivergent people, Jo Malone had an extremely heightened sense of smell, which in some situations might have been overwhelming. However, in her case, combined with her entrepreneurial ability to solve problems and to see things differently, her sense of smell made her uniquely qualified to craft and sell luxury candles and perfumes.

Understanding that someone's success might be because of their cognitive differences and not in spite of them is key to appreciating the different ways that we experience the world. By making adjustments that make certain environments more manageable for people with sensory processing issues, and by encouraging people to pursue their unique skills, we can make a huge difference.

Of course, for every person who manages to overcome the societal barriers to success faced by neurodivergent people, there are many more who aren't adequately supported. It is important to shift from focusing on the negatives to thinking about the positives, while never forgetting that there are adjustments people need to thrive. With adjustments, neurodivergent employees can be properly supported, which can enable them to flourish and even go beyond the neurotypical standard.

This idea can be expanded to relationships and friendships, too – if you are willing to make individualized adjustments for things such as communication and memory, you and your neurodivergent friend, partner or relative can enjoy a more meaningful relationship. There are many ways of doing this, but they all start with asking the individual what adaptations they need.

Sensory seeking

While sensory processing issues can often cause distress for people who are overwhelmed, it is worth bearing in mind that there is just as much joy to be found for people who are able to sensory seek.

Sensory seeking is any behaviour wherein you pursue stimulation through your senses: smelling candles, moving around, feeling nice fabrics. We all sensory seek in some way but, particularly for autistic people and those with ADHD, it can be necessary.

Sensory seeking is often called 'stimming', and those behaviours can look like rocking back and forth, feeling material and playing with their hands. These are behaviours that can be punished, particularly in controversial behavioural therapy, but understanding that it is not only normal but necessary and encouraging people to feel safe to engage in this behaviour will often make it easier for neurodivergent people to cope.

It's also important to remember that these are

behaviours many of us do – it is just often more noticeable in a neurodivergent person and more necessary for them.

HELPFUL ADAPTATIONS

One of the most helpful adaptations you can make for a neurodivergent person with reflective processing is to wait for up to ten seconds for them to respond; try to be conscious that not everyone is able to answer questions instantly.

Being mindful of differences in sensory processing is vitally important too: when someone tells you that they perceive a fluorescent light as flashing, do believe them, even if it isn't flashing for you!

If we all approach interactions with greater patience and awareness of people's different styles of communication and processing, neurodivergent people who experience challenges in these areas will feel better understood and supported.

ψ KEY TAKEAWAYS

- Many neurodivergent individuals have differences in processing information and sensory input, and may have more reflective processing speeds.

- Having patience and allowing people more time to process and understand information can help people with reflective processing.

- Sensory overwhelm might cause distress or meltdown and is not something that an individual can 'get used' to.

- Overwhelm can be prevented in some instances by removing labels from clothing, avoiding unpleasant textures, wearing ear defenders or noise-cancelling headphones, or turning down bright lights.

- Some neurodivergent people also sensory seek, which is also known as 'stimming'. Allowing individuals to feel safe in engaging in these behaviours makes it easier for them to cope with sensory differences.

ᴪ REFLECTION POINTS

- What are the benefits of both reflective and super-fast processing?

- How can you show sensitivity in relation to a neurodivergent person's sensory processing?

CHAPTER 4

WORKING MEMORY

Working memory is an area that a lot of neurodivergent people can struggle with. It essentially refers to the amount of information you can hold in your brain and use. It might impact your ability to problem-solve, make decisions and follow verbal instructions.

For example, you might go to the kitchen to make a drink, boil the kettle, and once you walk away you forget you need to make the tea. Maybe a simple task like putting the laundry on takes two or three tries, as you forget why you entered the room. You might go upstairs to get a book but forget the purpose of your trip after you get distracted by shutting a window because it's raining!

Difficulties with working memory can also affect

neurodivergent people when they meet new people. I often find I forget people's names, as their name may be the least interesting thing about them. I might remember where they are from, or the job they do or a funny story they told me, but my memory of their name just slips away!

Issues with working memory can be the reason why a lot of neurodivergent people might interrupt people when they are speaking. When they are having a conversation that is moving quickly they may have an idea, and if they don't share it immediately it will float out of their consciousness.

Working memory is important for decision-making but it is often unfairly seen as a reflection of someone's competence. Someone with difficulties with working memory might just need more reminders at home or at work to help them follow through with tasks. They might also have excellent memory in other areas – for example, some autistic people can have long-term and photographic memory that is far better than average.

Working memory can also impact your ability to take in verbal instructions. Due to my ADHD, I have difficulty with my working memory, and I sometimes struggle to follow and remember directions.

For instance, I often find myself needing to ask strangers how to get somewhere and then struggling to mentally retain the directions that I'm given! I could be told,

'Come out of Victoria Station, turn right, you will find a Sainsbury's on the corner, just after that turn left, and then take the second right after the bridge and you are there', and I will often only remember the first part of this verbal instruction.

As a consequence, I have to continuously ask people how to get to my destination until I arrive – and, yes, I know that Google Maps exists, but I struggle with map reading too!

In contrast, someone with good working memory might be able to hold all that directional information in their mind without getting distracted or forgetting what they are doing. In my case, I am not even listening to most of the directions you are giving me; I am simply holding on to that first instruction (whilst smiling and nodding at you!) as I try to remember it.

These cognitive differences might make a neurodivergent person appear rude or forgetful, and they might be misjudged because of them.

For example, if someone realizes you haven't remembered their name, they might be offended or hurt. However, it is important to remember that with the right tools, such as a smartphone with maps and the ability to set reminders, that person could be far less hindered out in the world. And, as the author Maxine Frances Roper's experiences reflect, if a neurodivergent person's issues with working memory

are misinterpreted as a sign that they are rude or careless, it can be distressing for them too:

> I was picked on at school for being clumsy and have mostly forgotten or come to terms with it. I still have traumatic flashbacks all the time to adult rows arising from my lack of short-term memory. I've been singled out and disbelieved to tears over it, at work and at home.

Maxine Frances Roper, *author with dyspraxia and ADHD (personal communication, November 2021)*

I have heard phrases like 'It goes in one ear and out the other' that reflect how we view people with working memory issues. If you have ever said something similar about a child or someone you work with, know that their difficulties with retaining information are probably connected to working memory in some way.

If you experience difficulties with processing and working memory, this can affect your planning and organization, which can also create problems and friction with other people. People with ADHD are often seen to fidget or doodle when people are speaking to them, which again can be interpreted as rude, but it can be a way to aid working memory and listening skills, keeping the body stimulated so the mind can focus.

HELPFUL ADAPTATIONS

If you know someone who struggles with working memory, there are various ways you can support them. One approach that can be effective is to provide gentle reminders using visual aids such as whiteboards.

To reduce my own difficulties with working memory, I love using magic white paper that you can stick on walls with static, and then I write things I need to remember to do or places that I need to be! Or sometimes I try to trigger my memory by leaving a relevant object by the door, such as a milk carton to remind myself I need to buy more milk!

Often, simply being patient when you have to repeat things to someone can be helpful. Make sure you allow some extra time if somebody needs a moment to write down instructions, and be understanding if they ask further questions. It can also be helpful to reflect on how you ask questions and to check for understanding; try to give instructions calmly with pauses, allow someone time to take notes and aim to be non-judgemental if they need to record something you say.

ψ KEY TAKEAWAYS

- Working memory refers to the amount of information you can hold in your brain and use.

- Difficulties with working memory can affect problem-solving, decision-making and following instructions.

- Gentle reminders, repeating information and being patient can help support people with working memory difficulties.

ψ REFLECTION POINTS

- Have you ever thought someone was rude for forgetting your name? Does understanding more about difficulties with working memory make you reconsider your reaction?

- Can you think of any ways you can support a neurodivergent person who struggles with working memory?

CHAPTER 5

COMMUNICATION

When you think of communication, it is likely that you only think in terms of talking to another person. However, there are many different types of communication: non-verbal communication, which includes body language, facial expressions, eye contact and sign language; visual communication; written communication; and listening.

We might judge a person who can't express themselves verbally or who struggles to listen to others as being a bad communicator, but it's often not the case.

A deaf person who can lip-read and speak through sign language is a great communicator in the right contexts, but they might struggle to converse with people who don't make an effort to pay attention or to learn sign language. A non-verbal autistic person with a text-to-speech machine or who paints beautiful pictures is still communicating. *The Reason I Jump* (2013), the vivid bestselling memoir of a 13-year-old non-verbal autistic boy, Naoki Higashida, was creatively composed using an alphabet grid.

There are other issues in communication for neurodivergent people, and these often relate as much to what people don't say as to what they do, particularly culturally. Recognizing what is generally considered to be an appropriate topic of conversation can be challenging for neurodivergent people. For example, in the UK, 'small talk' is considered an integral part of polite communication, yet there is no obvious logic to some small-talk exchanges, which may touch on relatively neutral topics such as the weather, work or your immediate surroundings.

At the National Autistic Society, when I specialized in supporting autistic jobseekers, a big part of my work was helping them to prepare for interviews. In my current role at Adjust, running training workshops for employers on recruitment and neurodiversity, I encourage employers to change their interview questions so that they aren't so confusing.

A seemingly simple opening question such as, 'Tell me about yourself' could be complicated for an autistic person to interpret, because they might think: 'Well, how much do you want to know about me? I'm not sure what to say?' If an employer changed the interview question to something more specific like, 'Tell me three skills and experiences you've had in your life that relate to this job', then that can make the interview process more accessible for autistic people.

The strikingly low levels of employment for autistic people (only 29 per cent of autistic people were in employment in the UK in the year ending June 2021, according to Office for National Statistics estimates (ONS, 2021)) highlight how important it is to make recruitment more neuro-inclusive. This is why I am so passionate about working with employers, because I feel like I can have a lasting impact on reducing the barriers autistic people may face during the recruitment process.

Consistency and reliability can be crucial for autistic people. It is very important in your interactions with an autistic person to do exactly what you say you're going to do. Whether you've scheduled a work meeting, planned a date or arranged to meet for a coffee, if you tell an autistic person you'll be there at 2 p.m., be there at 2 p.m. Change and uncertainty can be overwhelming for autistic people, and ensuring that you communicate properly and commit to pre-arranged times and dates can make a huge difference.

Additionally, while an autistic person might struggle to convey ideas verbally, preparation can be key to making

them feel comfortable in a new situation. For example, employers can offer to send questions to an autistic person in advance of an interview so they can process what will be asked and prepare answers.

Communication can be different in different settings too. Greta Thunberg, the young climate activist, is autistic and has ADHD (Elizabeth, 2021). I was asked in a neurodiversity workshop how Greta could be autistic if she could deliver speeches in front of the United Nations. But for a lot of autistic people, it might be easier to do a pre-rehearsed and scripted talk in front of 500 people than to have a one-to-one conversation with somebody.

In that one-on-one setting, there's a lot of nuanced communication taking place such as body language, navigating turn-taking and changing topics, which can all be quite difficult. These dynamic forms of communication might not come so naturally to some autistic people, while doing a scripted speech might suit them better.

I find it fascinating that because the person asking the question considered autism to be a negative neurotype they didn't think an autistic person could do something that they themselves would find hard. Neurodivergent individuals are often judged by neurotypical standards.

Thunberg, as a young autistic woman, has probably done more to raise awareness of climate change than any organization I've ever known. However, if she had applied for a job at a climate change organization before she was famous, she might not have made it through the interview process due to the rigidity of that environment. From this example, we can extrapolate that many organizations are likely to be missing out on a great deal of talent by always recruiting in the same way for the same skills and standards.

I am currently working with many organizations who are at the start of their neurodiversity conversation, and they are examining their recruitment methods to understand where there may be barriers for neurodivergent candidates. This makes me hopeful that over the next ten years we will start to see a significant increase in the numbers of neurodivergent people recruited, retained and supported in their professional development by workplaces.

DIFFERENT STYLES OF COMMUNICATION

Some neurodivergent people, especially those who struggle with communicating in writing, might be fantastic talkers and charismatic conversationalists, but it is important to be patient when it comes to the different ways someone might communicate.

For those with 'flat affect', whose tone and pitch might

not change depending on their emotions, social conversations can be difficult as they worry about being misinterpreted. There is a simple way we can all help to ease that discomfort: by listening to the words that people say and understanding that even if their tone seems flat, they may still be excited or happy. Dismissing them as 'cold', 'blunt' or 'rude' is hurtful and can only hinder communication.

Similarly, try not to assume that someone is being rude, or that they seem untrustworthy because they don't make eye contact when they are talking to you. For many neurodivergent people, particularly some autistic people, forcing themselves to make eye contact can be a distressing experience and is sometimes even painful, whereas they feel better able to focus and listen to you if they don't look you in the eyes. I have been told by autistic people that making eye contact can be as unbearable as staring into the sun.

Many neurodivergent people will in fact be listening to you more effectively if they are not looking at you! Perceptions of the value of eye contact may be different for autistic people too; an autistic person once asked me, 'Why should I make eye contact? You don't sit and stare at the radio when it is on.' That old phrase 'Look me in the eyes when I'm talking to you' is not always helpful!

Some autistic people can be very direct in a way that

neurotypical people might find rude, but often it can make life easier for everyone to be a little more direct.

A neurotypical person might say that they are OK when they're not, anticipating that the person they are speaking to might be able to intuit that it isn't the case. However, if you are talking to an autistic person who has difficulty interpreting tone, facial expressions or hints, they might just take you at your word. In a work setting, a question such as, 'Would you like to come to this meeting?', when there's no appropriate answer but 'yes', could be difficult for an autistic person to translate.

There are two easy ways to simplify interactions with autistic people: by understanding that someone isn't rude just because they're direct, and also by being direct in what you ask of people, especially in social situations and in the workplace.

COMMUNICATION CONTEXTS

For companies to become more neuro-inclusive, their recruitment processes need to evolve to meet the different needs of neurodivergent people. Interviews can be quite discriminatory for many neurodivergent individuals for several reasons.

For example, if you've got a working memory issue and someone asks you a question such as, 'Tell me about a time you had a conflict at work; how did you resolve this and what did you learn from it?', you might feel overwhelmed by what you are being asked to recall because there are three separate parts to that question. Communication issues affecting neurodivergent people may also arise at assessment centres or when they are filling out application forms.

Managers need to have greater awareness of the hurdles presented by rigid recruitment processes as a more flexible approach to recruitment can have huge benefits for neurodivergent employees.

At interview stage, a lot of value is placed on the first impression you develop of a person. You might be thinking about how confidently they can get their points across, how much eye contact they make or how natural their tone of voice seems. Even if you aren't deliberately looking out for these things, they can all impact the idea of an individual that you form in your mind. Biases such as these will always put those with communication differences at a disadvantage.

If somebody seems like the right fit for the role, but you are put off by their lack of eye contact, or think that they lack confidence or sound 'flat' in their tone of voice, or perhaps they seem to 'jump' around between topics, it is important to remember that these things are not a reflection of the individual or their abilities. It is most likely that they are concentrating on formulating the right answer and collecting their thoughts, rather than working hard on masking their communication differences. You can miss out on a great deal of talent if you place too much value on conversational fluency, confidence and communication.

The workshops we run with recruiters, managers and colleagues are the key to starting to unlock neurodivergent potential. But, from the perspective of neurodivergent employees, they also need to know that they've got their own pathway of support in the workplace. *Is there a neurodiversity network? Do they understand their own neurotype?*

Educational settings can also be a challenging context for neurodivergent people with communication differences. For example, autistic children in a busy classroom may not respond to a teacher's instruction unless they are named personally. An autistic child may more effectively follow a task or instruction when they are directly addressed and the teacher's expectations of them are individually clarified.

A teacher's first impression may be that a student does not seem to hear them (many undiagnosed autistic children get wrongly referred to audiology departments) or is wilfully refusing to follow instructions. However, once you use an autistic child's name to engage with them, the communication process can be much less confusing for them.

HELPFUL ADAPTATIONS

Respecting communication differences and responding to them in a non-judgemental way will help to put neurodivergent people at greater ease during social interactions.

Addressing people directly by name, simplifying questions within conversations and sticking to pre-arranged commitments to reduce uncertainty can all enhance communication with neurodivergent people too.

It is important to remember that many of the adjustments discussed in this chapter can improve the environment for everyone! Who doesn't benefit from clear communication?

ᛉ KEY TAKEAWAYS

- There are many different forms of communication including verbal communication, non-verbal communication, visual communication, written communication and listening.

- Some neurodivergent people struggle in a world based on neurotypical conventions around communication.

- Difficulties with communication can affect

neurodivergent people's employment opportunities, educational experiences and social lives.

● Simple adaptations and increased understanding can improve neurodivergent people's experiences of communication.

Ψ REFLECTION POINTS

● How can you try to communicate more effectively with neurodivergent friends, relatives or colleagues?

● Does having greater awareness about neurodiversity make you reflect differently on a time when you may have judged somebody negatively for the way they communicated with you?

CHAPTER 6

UNWRITTEN RULES

One of the biggest challenges a neurodivergent person, particularly an autistic person, might experience with communication is unwritten rules. Unwritten rules are a set of cultural expectations that are assumed to be understood by everyone based on the misconception that we all have the same shared experiences and values.

I have worked with many autistic people in the workplace who have been ostracized, bullied or nearly lost their jobs because they struggled to follow unwritten rules. These rules could be things such as offering to make other people a cup of tea when you make yourself one, staying late to meet a deadline or not asking questions that are perceived to be personal.

UNWRITTEN RULES

1. Text your date back (but not right away)

2. 'Do you want to get up and teach the class yourself?' (Don't actually get up and do it)

3. Work from home if you like (but not every day)

4. Party starts at 8 (arrive at 8:30)

5. My door is always open (at these specific times)

Failure to follow these rules is often disapproved of and neurotypical people often assume that these social norms are implicit. By simply voicing these rules out loud and not presuming that they are obvious, you ensure everyone is on a level playing field. In fact, it can be worth questioning why some of these rules exist at all.

Unwritten rules can often change without warning in different contexts, and they're often cultural. For example, in the UK, we love to queue. We queue in many different contexts: for a table at a restaurant, to use public toilets or to pay for our groceries in a supermarket. But we don't typically queue in pubs and bars, where it is often a free-for-all. It can be tough to know when it's right to queue, and it's not always considered acceptable to ask.

When I worked at a university as a disability adviser, the international students officer used to run sessions on British culture. As these sessions also helped my autistic students to learn about unwritten rules, I used to ask if they could attend too.

MISUNDERSTANDINGS

Once, a woman I supported called in sick at work. She took a few hours to rest, watched a bit of *This Morning* and slept in, but because she felt better in the afternoon, she went to work at 2 p.m. She was logical, dedicated and loyal and wanted to get back to work, but her manager saw her as someone who wanted a lie-in and who thought she could turn up when she wanted.

His view was that when you're sick, you're off for the day, even if you feel better. This kind of unwritten rule can be tough to navigate and it is important that neurotypical managers don't assume someone's intentions without further discussion.

MASKING

Difficulties with unwritten rules are common in the workplace, but they often manifest socially too.

Women and girls are often not diagnosed as autistic early in life, because a lot of young boys can have more apparent behavioural issues that lead to diagnosis (Ploszajski, 2019). Girls are socialized to hide their difficulties and to conform to social expectations as much as possible, so they 'mask', hiding their true selves and trying to blend in. I have spoken to autistic women who explained that when they were at school, they would study the personality of someone popular in the class and mimic it.

Socially, this can make life very painful for autistic girls. There are unwritten social rules that are never explained, and girls who fail to follow them are often bullied and excluded. As they often aren't diagnosed, they don't understand why they're different, which is very painful.

Girls, rather than communicating an issue directly or by bullying in the violent ways boys often do, often engage in 'covert bullying', such as gossiping or leaving someone out. This is harder for an autistic girl to pick up on, but it also makes it easier to hide the bullying from oblivious teachers.

Autistic girls are often targeted by people who pretend to be their friends, with the intention of using them as a source of amusement. Neurodiversity advocate Siena Castellon describes her experiences of covert bullying:

> When I was 12, a group of girls, who claimed to be my friends, insisted that I wear a panda onesie to the school Christmas dance. They told me that they would be wearing animal onesies too. I believed them. Luckily, my mom intervened and made me wear a party dress. When I got to the dance, the girls were wearing party dresses and were visibly disappointed that I hadn't come to the dance dressed like a panda.
>
> **Siena Castellon,** *author (Castellon, 2020, p.200)*

Masking and trying desperately to fit in might enable

girls to cope until they're about 13 or 14 years old, but then, when relationships get more complicated, this starts to break down. This might be the point where they display behavioural issues, for example, self-harm, shoplifting and other rebellious behaviour.

I have worked with girls who been diagnosed with oppositional defiant disorder (ODD), a behaviour disorder in which children can be seen as being uncooperative and defiant towards figures of authority, such as parents or teachers (Mayo Clinic, 2022). Autistic women and girls can also be mistakenly diagnosed with borderline personality disorder, obsessive compulsive disorder (OCD), anxiety and other conditions. This is a major issue.

There will be women in the workplace who are autistic and undiagnosed, and the internalizing, masking and mirroring of behaviour that they do on a day-to-day basis can be both damaging and exhausting. A lot of behavioural therapy, which is highly controversial, will encourage masking, but it shouldn't be celebrated. I believe that people should be accepted for who they really are.

These rules and this pressure to mask can also pop up in romantic situations, such as what to do and what not to do on a first date. However, while people can hide who they are for so long, their psychological distress will only grow as they try to hide.

People are often ostracized for not understanding unwritten rules, particularly in British culture, which can be exceptionally passive-aggressive. Looking at the rules you follow and reflecting on whether they could be less rigid could make a massive difference to the way you communicate with other people, whether they're neurodivergent or not. Honesty can only strengthen communication.

Greta Thunberg said that she appreciates being autistic because 'Being different is a gift. It makes me see things from outside the box. I don't easily fall for lies, I can see through things' (*BBC Newsround*, 2019). While autistic people, especially girls, struggle to cope in social situations that are rife with unwritten rules and complex behavioural codes, they often thrive in spaces where those masks can be dropped.

When people find friends, hobbies or workplaces that celebrate and embrace who they are, and make an effort to meet them halfway, life gets a lot easier – in fact, early diagnosis can seriously mitigate the risk of the dangerous behaviours mentioned in this chapter.

HELPFUL ADAPTATIONS

Always try to tolerate neurodivergent people's differences and not to simply assume that they share common views and experiences. This can reduce misunderstandings about unwritten rules and distress related to feelings of falling short of social expectations.

Within your workplace, school or community, if you notice someone struggling to grasp social norms, attempt to clearly communicate the 'rules' that might confuse them.

ψ KEY TAKEAWAYS

- Unwritten rules are a common challenge for neurodivergent people, particularly autistic people, but the same individuals can thrive when they don't have to mask their difficulties.

- People are often viewed negatively for failing to follow unwritten rules or social norms. Greater tolerance may help to reduce the challenges experienced by neurodivergent people who find unwritten rules hard to understand.

ψ REFLECTION POINTS

- Can you think of some 'unwritten rules' in your society? How obvious do you think they are?

- How can you support someone who seems unaware of unwritten rules?

CHAPTER 7

EMOTIONS

Emotions can be a tricky subject for neurodivergent people for many different reasons. For a start, when you experience the world differently from other people or perhaps have difficulty communicating with others, emotional subjects can be tricky to navigate.

There are other issues too. People with ADHD, for example, might have emotional dysregulation, wherein they struggle to control and regulate feelings (ADHD Aware, 2021). A relatively minor incident might set off what appears on the outside to be a temper tantrum, or they might struggle with feelings of rejection or disappointment.

Autistic people often have to deal with challenging situations in a social world organized around neurotypical

people's needs, and end up having meltdowns, which
is when their senses get so overwhelmed they literally
stop being able to function properly.

EMOTIONAL REGULATION

There are specific terms for the difficulties expressing,
identifying or regulating emotions that are experienced
by many neurodivergent people, wherever they fall
under the umbrella. Alexithymia, for example, is when
someone cannot identify or name their own emotions.
A neurodivergent person might know that they're
feeling something but find it tough to articulate it to an
outsider. This can be really distressing, particularly if it is
a painful emotion (Wilkinson, n.d.).

Additionally, many autistic people struggle with
interoception, the perception of sensations from within
the body. This is the sense that most people have that
tells them if they are hungry, are in pain or need to go to
the bathroom, for example. Struggling to recognize those
needs – or articulate them – can also affect emotional
regulation, causing burnout and meltdowns in people
who are unable to give their body what it needs.

A difficulty with managing and expressing feelings
can lead to the misunderstanding that some people,
particularly autistic people, don't actually *feel* emotions

– they do, but naming and expressing them can be harder.

This is what leads to the myth that autistic people are lacking in empathy – they are not, and many are hyper-empathetic. They just have more difficulty understanding what they are feeling and knowing the 'right' way to express it. This can also lead to overwhelm and burnout when an autistic person experiences all-consuming emotion and empathy but doesn't know how to pinpoint or manage it.

MANAGING FEELINGS OF DIFFERENCE

There are social reasons that exacerbate intense and difficult emotions for neurodivergent people. A lot of neurodivergent people will have very high anxiety and low confidence. It's not surprising if, at every turn, you try to do something and you struggle at it or find it very difficult.

Many neurodivergent people will have experienced repeated criticism for failing to meet neurotypical standards of behaviour or following unwritten rules. For some people with ADHD, particularly those who experience the intense emotional sensitivity known as rejection sensitive dysphoria (RSD), such criticism can feel almost unbearable (Dodson, 2022).

Restlessness can be part of ADHD, and keeping to routines can be challenging for people with ADHD. They might thrive by following an established routine, but it can be quite difficult to get that routine in place and stick to it. The frustration that someone might feel with themselves when they get things wrong can be very extreme and overwhelming.

Additionally, feeling ostracized, bullied or different can often lead to feelings of extreme hurt or anger that might be hard to express appropriately. With support, diagnosis and understanding, neurodivergent people can learn to channel their emotions.

On the flipside, experiencing high emotions isn't necessarily negative; people who are neurodivergent are often incredibly loving, open and empathetic. They can be also very passionate and charismatic and throw themselves into their interests with abandon. Not everyone with ADHD can do this, but I often say that ADHD is two sides of the same coin and most people with ADHD are very outcome-focused and some are excellent in business and target-driven roles.

ACCEPTING EMOTIONAL DIFFERENCES

In social or romantic situations, the way that neurodivergent people express their feelings can cause friction with people who don't understand their emotional differences.

For example, a person with ADHD might not reach out to a friend for several weeks; perhaps they have been distracted or busy. However, their friend might find their lack of communication strange and think that they have stopped wanting to maintain the friendship. The answer, as always, is to communicate and to understand that people might have different love languages.

Something such as ADHD, autism or dyslexia is innate in who you are – while unfortunately some people might see this as a hindrance, it is a fundamental part of personal identity. There is no cure for these conditions, and while some neurotypical people think there should be, a cure would change who a person is at their core. Instead, neurodivergent people need understanding and adjustments so they can thrive and experience full acceptance of who they are.

ADHD is the only one of the four neurotypes we focus on in this guide for which medication is prescribed for the neurotype – often in the form of stimulants that increase activity in certain parts of the brain. Many people with neurodivergent brains may take medication for other overlapping conditions such as anxiety, depression, sleep and epilepsy, but ADHD is the only neurotype that has specific medication.

I once heard someone liken the symptoms of ADHD to a pollen allergy. If you were allergic to pollen, you wouldn't walk through a massive field without taking an antihistamine. He explained that life is so stimulating for him, with sensory overload and racing thoughts, that his medication enables him to focus.

However, other people find that ADHD medication alters their sense of who they really are, and they don't feel like they have the same levels of passion, creativity, hyper-focus and energy when they take it. For author Maxine Frances Roper, ADHD medication helps her to write more creatively:

ADHD medication helps me get to the sweet spot where I have the feelings and ideas to be creative, without being so overwhelmed by feelings and ideas that I can't physically sit down and organize them into a piece of work.

Maxine Frances Roper, author with ADHD and dyspraxia (personal communication, November 2021)

HELPFUL ADAPTATIONS

Supporting someone who struggles with regulating emotions and feelings can sometimes be as simple as offering friendly reminders: Have they eaten? What do they need to feel OK today? Would it be helpful to go for a walk?

At other times it can be as straightforward as just being understanding: Can they tell you about their feelings in their own way, maybe visually or in a way that isn't too strenuous?

Ultimately, we need to understand that everyone is different, and be patient – the fact that someone struggles to articulate their feelings doesn't mean they don't have any!

ψ KEY TAKEAWAYS

- Many neurodivergent people struggle identifying and/or regulating emotions.

- Difficulty understanding or naming an emotion is particularly common in autism and is known as alexithymia.

- Many autistic people also struggle with interoception and can find it hard to gauge signals such as hunger and fullness, tiredness and needing to use the bathroom.

- Intense emotions are also common in neurodivergent people. This means that many neurodivergent people are extremely empathetic, passionate and caring.

Ψ REFLECTION POINTS

- How can you offer feedback as constructively as possible to support neurodivergent people who may be hyper-sensitive to criticism?

- Can you think of different ways that people might feel and express empathy?

CHAPTER 8

PROBLEM-SOLVING

One year, a few days before Christmas, I was sitting with a young boy while his mum was getting him to write out Christmas cards. They weren't spelt correctly because of his dyslexia, and because of his dyspraxia, his handwriting was messy. His mum was making him write them again and again and it was frustrating. It probably took 45 minutes of tears and anger, his negative emotions rising up as the minutes passed.

Later in the afternoon, after his mum had taped Christmas decorations up, the boy said they should invent superglue tape because when you Sellotape stuff up and then put the heating on, Sellotape dries up. His creativity was the result of him having the verbal skills

and the problem-solving ability to originate ideas and be creative, and his mum just said, 'Whatever'.

I'm not being critical of parents, but I said to her later that we should have got him to make a poster for superglue Sellotape to sell it. Then, as her son grows up, she could refer to his brilliant ideas to explain to him that his dyslexia and dyspraxia profile isn't just the stuff he can't do. It is also his inventive brain.

CELEBRATING NEURODIVERGENT SKILLS

A lot of neurodivergent people are great problem-solvers because they often have one of two key skills: out-of-the-box thinking and logical problem-solving. That boy I met is an out-of-the-box thinker, and that's something that could serve him well if he finds the right kind of career path.

Skills like these are hugely beneficial in STEM and the arts. Pattern recognition is another ability that is common in some neurodivergent people. Patterns are everywhere in nature, and an innate ability to recognize and understand them is undervalued.

And things are changing. Many organizations, including GCHQ, are now actively recruiting dyslexic and neurodivergent people because of their strengths such as pattern recognition, creative thinking and problem-solving.

I recently trained an organization that embraced diversity and inclusion, adjusting their recruitment process to recruit from more diverse talent pools. This employer had created an environment where people could be their authentic selves – while I was visiting their office, somebody skipped through reception with their shoes and socks off. I don't know if that person was neurodivergent or not, but I was impressed that they felt comfortable enough in that environment to behave exactly how they wanted.

A lot of autistic people, along with all neurodivergent profiles, have significantly contrasting abilities. They may have areas of outstanding strength and other areas where they need support or adjustments. There's a bit of a stereotype that all autistic people excel at maths or IT, but I have worked with an incredibly broad range of people throughout my career, and I have seen autistic people do well at a variety of jobs.

One thing that many people I have worked with have in common is a good eye for detail. Sometimes that might be manifested in an ability to notice other people's mistakes: in copyediting, for example. A lot of autistic people describe mistakes as jumping out at them. If I read a document, especially if I have written it, my brain goes into survival mode, and I don't see any mistakes, but someone who is autistic may look at the same document and immediately notice errors.

In diagnostic tests for dyslexia, many dyslexic people score highly in problem-solving, and a lot of dyslexic and autistic people score highly in verbal reasoning. Dyslexic people can also be very intuitive and good with people.

When I was employed at a medical school, I worked with different groups of medical healthcare professionals, and several of the physiotherapists had dyslexia. This is because their strengths, such as their verbal skills, problem-solving, ability to work well with people and 3D thinking (visualizing something in your mind and turning it around) made them well suited to their profession.

A lot of dyslexic people really see the big picture, and we need people who think that way. For example, if you go to the doctor with a bad foot, a physiotherapist would be able to take a holistic approach and tell you that you need to increase your core strength, or that the problem comes from the way you walk. This ability to look beyond the small details and to think outside the box perfectly illustrates the idea that we need all kinds of different thinkers, and this attitude is core to understanding neurodiversity.

The high proportion of architects who are dyslexic, including the late Richard Rogers, who designed London's Millennium Dome and Paris's Centre Pompidou (The Yale Center for Dyslexia and Creativity, 2017), perhaps also reflects the skills of many dyslexic people in the areas of problem-solving, spatial awareness and pattern recognition.

ᴪ KEY TAKEAWAYS

- Many neurodivergent people are brilliant problem-solvers due to their creative, out-of-the-box thinking styles.

- Excellent pattern recognition and logical-thinking skills are common in neurodivergent people, particularly autistic people.

- Many organizations are now actively seeking to recruit dyslexic and other neurodivergent people due to associated strengths in problem-solving and pattern recognition.

- Contrasting profiles of ability are common in neurodivergent people, in which areas of outstanding strength coexist with areas where further support is needed.

Ψ REFLECTION POINTS

- How can out-of-the-box thinking be useful to society?

- Can you think of ways that neurodivergent people's distinctive skills could enhance your workplace, school or community?

CONCLUSION

I hope that this guide has galvanized your interest in neurodiversity and helped you to develop your understanding of some of the key concepts.

If you feel better placed to celebrate the power of thinking differently now than when you started reading, I have achieved one of my goals. We have focused on four neurotypes to illustrate the concept of neurodiversity, but there are many other neurotypes out there too – perhaps they can be discussed in *The Pocket Guide to Neurodiversity Part Two*!

My main aim is to raise awareness of the many children and adults who do not think in a neurotypical way, and of the ways in which these neurodivergent people can be disabled by the neurotypical structures we have in our society.

This is just the start of your journey, and I hope that your understanding of neurodiversity continues to grow. Within society, understanding is gradually increasing, in part due to the hard work of activists who raise awareness of how neurodivergence presents and affects individuals. This has led to an increase in diagnoses of conditions such as ADHD and autism, particularly in groups that were once overlooked, such as women and girls.

But even more needs to be done for different groups, including people of colour. Greater understanding of the different ways people may present, as well as the positive traits that neurodivergence can give someone, means that a person will have an easier time accessing support and being accepted.

It is important to remember that, while things are far better for neurodivergent people than they were even ten years ago, there are still many barriers to overcome. Education and employment are often organized around a neurotypical framework, while navigating an overloaded healthcare system can make diagnosis difficult to access. Additionally, widespread stereotypes and misconceptions about more stigmatized neurodivergent conditions, such as autism, can make it difficult for a person to navigate society and engage with people on a social level.

To return to my cactus metaphor in Chapter 1, sometimes simple environmental adjustments are all that are needed to enable someone to thrive. These adjustments can be simple: understanding why someone is often late, offering different coloured backgrounds on documents, challenging your assumptions if someone doesn't make eye contact.

Everyone is different, and every neurodivergent condition is too, but by communicating with people on an individual basis, you can find out exactly what they need. This will make life easier not only for neurodivergent people but for everyone – wouldn't a more holistic approach improve wellbeing for every person?

The tips and information in this introductory book will support you in developing your understanding of neurodiversity and adjusting to a neurodivergent framework of approaching the world, so that you can start to make the world more inclusive by simply paying attention to people around you.

NEURODIVERSITY RESOURCES

BOOKS

Adam Feinstein (2018) *Autism Works: A Guide to Successful Employment*. Abingdon, UK: Routledge.

Brock Eide and Fernette Eide (2011) *The Dyslexic Advantage: Unlocking the Hidden Potential of the Dyslexic Brain*. London: Hay House UK.

David Grant, (2017) *That's the Way I Think: Dyslexia, Dyspraxia and ADHD Explained*. Abingdon, UK: Routledge.

Dr Gabor Maté (2019) *Scattered Minds: The Origins and Healing of Attention Deficit Disorder*. London: Vermillion.

Janet Taylor and Mary Morris (2015) *Dyspraxia: Dyspraxic Adults Surviving in a Non-Dyspraxic World: A Dyspraxia Foundation Adult Support Group Publication.* Hitchin, UK: Dyspraxia Foundation.

Judy Singer (2017) *NeuroDiversity: The Birth of an Idea.* Self published.

Mark Haddon (2004) *The Curious Incident of the Dog in the Night-Time.* London: Vintage.

Temple Grandin (2014) *The Autistic Brain: Thinking Across the Spectrum.* London: Rider.

Thomas Armstrong (2011) *The Power of Neurodiversity: Unleashing the Advantages of Your Differently Wired Brain.* Boston, MA: Da Capo Lifelong Books.

Victoria Honeybourne (2019) *The Neurodiverse Workplace: An Employer's Guide to Managing and Working with Neurodivergent Employees, Clients and Customers.* London: Jessica Kingsley Publishers.

DOCUMENTARIES

Chris Packham: Asperger's and Me

Chris Packham invites us inside his autistic world to try to show what it is like being him. Chris explores the questions of whether Asperger's has helped make him who he is today.

Kara Tointon: Don't Call Me Stupid

Actress Kara Tointon presents a documentary about dyslexia and meets other dyslexic people whose moving stories reveal the impact it can have on young lives without the right support.

MEDIA

Dyspraxic Me: www.youtube.com/watch?v=dEIwafUGgnY

Desert Island Discs with Jo Malone:
www.bbc.co.uk/programmes/b04xmqd6

Is ADHD an Advantage?
www.youtube.com/watch?v=n2EVEYmeSqg

Things Not to Say to an Autistic Person:
www.youtube.com/watch?v=d69tTXOvRq4

Things Not to Say to Someone with Dyslexia:
www.youtube.com/watch?v=ObwAzZr87jg&t=1s

PODCASTS

Neurodiversity – The New Normal (The Different Minds Podcast)

The Neurodiversity Podcast with Emily Kircher-Morris

Neurodiversity – Eliminating Kryptonite & Enabling Superheroes

REFERENCES

Preface

ACAS (n.d.) *Neurodiversity in the Workplace*. London: Advisory, Conciliation and Arbitration Service. Accessed on 16/05/2022 at https://webarchive.nationalarchives.gov.uk/ukgwa/20210104113255/https://archive.acas.org.uk/index.aspx?articleid=6676

ONS (2021) *Outcomes for Disabled People in the UK: 2021*. London: Office of National Statistics. Accessed on 16/05/2022 at www.ons.gov.uk/peoplepopulationandcommunity/healthandsocialcare/disability/articles/outcomesfordisabledpeopleintheuk/2021

Chapter 1

ACAS (n.d.) *Neurodiversity in the Workplace.* London: Advisory, Conciliation and Arbitration Service. Accessed on 16/05/2022 at https://webarchive.nationalarchives.gov.uk/ukgwa/20210104113255/https://archive.acas.org.uk/index.aspx?articleid=6676

Blume, H. (1998) 'Neurodiversity: On the neurological underpinnings of geekdom.' *The Atlantic.* Accessed on 06/09/2022 at https://www.theatlantic.com/magazine/archive/1998/09/neurodiversity/305909

GCHQ (2021) *Dyslexic Thinking Skills Are Mission Critical for Protecting the Country.* Cheltenham, UK: Government Communication Headquarters. Accessed on 16/05/2022 at www.gchq.gov.uk/news/dyslexic-thinking-skills

Miah, S. (2021) *Living a World of Difference.* London: Newham Voices. Accessed on 16/05/2022 at https://newhamvoices.co.uk/living-a-world-of-difference

Singer, J. (n.d.) *What Is Neurodiversity?* Reflections on Neurodiversity. Accessed on 16/05/2022 at https://neurodiversity2.blogspot.com/p/what.html

Chapter 2

ADHD UK (n.d.) *What Is ADHD?* ADHD UK. Accessed on 19/05/2022 at https://adhduk.co.uk/about-adhd

Archer, D. (2014) 'How ADHD puts athletes in the zone.'

Forbes. Accessed on 26/05/2022 at www.forbes.com/sites/dalearcher/2014/07/16/how-adhd-puts-athletes-in-the-zone/?sh=4dc0134813a3

Barnfield, K. (2021) 'Christine McGuinness: TV star "trying to be a bit more myself now" after "amazing" diagnosis of autism.' *Sky News*. Accessed on 26/05/2022 at https://news.sky.com/story/christine-mcguinness-tv-star-trying-to-be-a-bit-more-myself-now-after-amazing-diagnosis-of-autism-12485953

Battersby, K. (2018) 'Chris Packham reveals the reality of living with Asperger's – and his "romantic plan" to be reunited with his dogs after he dies.' *Radio Times*. Accessed on 19/05/2022 at www.radiotimes.com/tv/documentaries/chris-packham-reveals-the-reality-of-living-with-aspergers-and-his-romantic-plan-to-be-reunited-with-his-dogs-after-he-dies

BBC Yorkshire (2021) 'Dyspraxia: My life with the misunderstood condition.' *BBC*. Accessed on 19/05/2022 at www.bbc.co.uk/news/uk-england-57269137

BDA (2022) *Dyslexia*. Bracknell, UK: British Dyslexia Association. Accessed on 16/05/2022 at www.bdadyslexia.org.uk/dyslexia

Bedigan, M. (2022) 'Rory Bremner says ADHD is "my best friend and my worst enemy".' *Belfast Telegraph*. Accessed on 19/05/2022 at www.belfasttelegraph.co.uk/entertainment/film-tv/news/rory-bremner-says-adhd-is-my-best-friend-and-my-worst-enemy-41332120.html

Brown, L. (2022) *Identity-First Language*. Washington, DC: Autistic Self Advocacy Network. Accessed on 16/05/2022 at https://autisticadvocacy.org/about-asan/identity-first-language

CDC (2022) *Autism and Vaccines*. Atlanta: Centers for Disease Control and Prevention. Accessed on 16/05/2022 at https://pubmed.ncbi.nlm.nih.gov/10376617

Crompton, C.J., Ropar, D., Evans-Williams, C.V.M. et al. (2020) 'Autistic peer-to-peer information transfer is highly effective.' *Sage Journals* 24, 7, 1704–1712.

Dutton, J. (2021) *How Swimming Saved Michael Phelps: An ADHD Story*. ADDitude Magazine. Accessed on 16/05/2022 at www.additudemag.com/michael-phelps-adhd-advice-from-the-olympians-mom

Dyslexia.uk.com (2022) *What Is Dyslexia?* Dyslexia.uk.com. Accessed on 16/05/2022 at dyslexia.uk.com

Elder Robinson, J. (2009) *Look Me in the Eye*. London: Ebury.

Evening Standard (2008) 'Harry Potter: The brain disorder which means I can't tie my shoelaces.' *Evening Standard*. Accessed on 19/05/2022 at www.standard.co.uk/showbiz/harry-potter-the-brain-disorder-which-means-i-can-t-tie-my-shoelaces-6894945.html

Freeth, B. (2021) '15 celebrities describe what it's like living with ADHD as an adult.' *Cosmopolitan*. Accessed on 26/05/2022 at www.cosmopolitan.com/uk/body/health/g38300011/celebrities-adhd

Gannon, L. (2017) '"I don't regret the anger. I don't regret drinking. Life can be painful. That's the deal." In an exclusive interview with Event, Sir Antony Hopkins talks Hannibal Lecter, loathing luvvies and how at 80 he never forgets his lines.' *Daily Mail.* Accessed on 19/05/2022 at www.dailymail.co.uk/home/event/article-4587980/Anthony-Hopkins-Hannibal-Lecter-Transformers.html

Holland, K. (2012) 'Dyspraxia has good points – Florence.' *The Irish Times.* Accessed on 19/05/2022 at www.irishtimes.com/news/dyspraxia-has-good-points-florence-1.532002

Irlen (n.d.) *Reading Problems, Dyslexia, Learning Difficulties.* Irlen. Accessed on 06/09/2022 at https://irlen.com/reading-problems-dyslexia-learning-difficulties-the-irlen-method

Levine, N. (2019) 'The big read – Loyle Carner: "All the best things about me come from my ADHD".' *NME.* Accessed on 19/05/2022 at www.nme.com/big-reads/big-read-loyle-carner-interview-not-waving-but-drowning-2481201

Loomes, R., Hull, L. and Mandy, W.P.L. (2017) 'What is the male-to-female ration in autism spectrum disorder? A systematic review and meta-analysis.' *Journal of the American Academy of Child and Adolescent Psychiatry, 56,* 6, 466–474.

Mead, A. (2021) 'Ellis Genge.' *The Rugby Journal.* Accessed on 26/05/2022 at www.therugbyjournal.com/rugby-blog/ellis-genge

Milton, D. (2018) *The Double Empathy Problem.* London:

National Autistic Society. Accessed on 16/05/2022 at www. autism.org.uk/advice-and-guidance/professional-practice/ double-empathy

NAS (2022a) *Autistic Women and Girls.* London: National Autistic Society. Accessed on 16/05/2022 at www.autism.org. uk/advice-and-guidance/what-is-autism/autistic-women-and-girls

NAS (2022b) *Autism and Gender Identity.* London: National Autistic Society. Accessed on 16/05/2022 at www.autism. org.uk/advice-and-guidance/what-is-autism/autism-and-gender-identity

NAS (2022c) *The History of Autism.* London: National Autistic Society. Accessed on 16/05/2022 at www.autism.org.uk/ advice-and-guidance/what-is-autism/the-history-of-autism

Ojomu, N. (2019) 'Mel B opens up about living with ADHD as she uses nature and exercise to heal anxiety.' *Metro.* Accessed on 26/05/2022 at https://metro.co.uk/2019/07/25/ mel-b-opens-up-about-living-with-adhd-as-she-uses-nature-and-exercise-to-heal-anxiety-10458873

Olivardia, R. (2020) *The Dyslexia and ADHD Connection.* ADDitude Magazine. Accessed on 16/05/2022 at www. additudemag.com/adhd-dyslexia-connection

Pang, C. (2019). *Let's Be Super Human.* Camilla Pang. Accessed on 26/05/2022 at camillapang.com

Rodden, J. (2021) *Having ADHD and Taking Medicine for It Is*

Nothing to Be Ashamed of. ADDitude Magazine. Accessed on 16/05/2022 at https://www.additudemag.com/simone-biles-adhd-olympic-gymnast-publicly-addresses-condition

Sandman-Hurley, K. (2021) *The Adult Side of Dyslexia.* London: Jessica Kingsley Publishers.

SNL (2021, May 9). *Elon Musk Monologue – SNL* [Video]. YouTube. Accessed on 26/05/2022 at www.youtube.com/watch?v=fCF8I_X1qKI

Strombo (2013, 6 March). *Dan Aykroyd Talks Mental Health and Acting* [Video]. YouTube. Accessed on 26/05/2022 at www.youtube.com/watch?v=XftZWhTnveo

Taylor, B., Miller, E., Farrington, C.P., Petropoulos, M.C., Favot-Mayaud, I., Li, J. and Waight, P.A. (1999) 'Autism and measles, mumps, and rubella vaccine: no epidemiological evidence for a causal association.' *Lancet, June 12,* 353(9169), 2026–2029.

Tobin, A.M. (2008) 'Harry Potter star's disability takes cloak off DCD.' *The Globe and Mail.* Accessed on 19/05/2022 at www.theglobeandmail.com/life/harry-potter-stars-disability-takes-cloak-off-dcd/article20386836

Weintraub, S. (2008) 'Justin Timberlake interview – the Love Guru.' *Collider.* Accessed on 26/05/2022 at https://collider.com/justin-timberlake-interview-the-love-guru

Willingham, E. (2013) 'Wall Street' actress Daryl Hannah is an autistic woman.' *Forbes.* Accessed on 19/05/2022

at www.forbes.com/sites/emilywillingham/2013/09/29/
wall-street-actress-daryl-hannah-also-autistic-
woman/?sh=57edc68f49fa

Chapter 3

BBC News (2015) 'Jo Malone says childhood dyslexia helped
her to smell.' BBC. Accessed on 19/05/2022 at www.bbc.
co.uk/news/av/business-34769381

Castellon, S. (2020) The Spectrum Girl's Survival Guide: How
to Grow Up Awesome and Autistic. London: Jessica Kingsley
Publishers.

Magidoff, S. (2021) Carl Honoré. Slow Entrepreneur.
Accessed on 19/05/2022 at www.slowentrepreneur.com/the-
interviews/carl-honor

Chapter 4

Higashida, N. (2013) The Reason I Jump. Trans. K.A. Yoshida
and D. Mitchell. New York: Random House.

Chapter 5

Elizabeth, D. (2021) 'Greta Thunberg on her autism diagnosis
and climate activism.' Teen Vogue. Accessed on 26/05/2022
at www.teenvogue.com/story/greta-thunberg-autism-
diagnosis-climate-activism

ONS (2021) Outcomes for Disabled People in the UK: 2021.
Office for National Statistics. Accessed on 26/05/2022

at www.ons.gov.uk/peoplepopulationandcommunity/
healthandsocialcare/disability/articles/outcomesfordisabled
peopleintheuk/2021

Chapter 6

BBC Newsround (2019) 'Greta Thunberg: 16-year-old
climate activist inspired international youth movement.'
BBC. Accessed on 19/05/2022 at www.bbc.co.uk/
newsround/47467038

Castellon, S. (2020) *The Spectrum Girl's Survival Guide: How
to Grow Up Awesome and Autistic.* London: Jessica Kingsley
Publishers.

Mayo Clinic (2022) *Oppositional Defiant Disorder (ODD).*
Rochester, MN: Mayo Clinic. Accessed on 19/05/2022 at www.
mayoclinic.org/diseases-conditions/oppositional-defiant-
disorder/symptoms-causes/syc-20375831

Ploszajski, A. (2019) 'Women "better than men at disguising
autism symptoms".' *The Guardian*. Accessed on 26/05/2022
at www.theguardian.com/society/2019/sep/13/women-
better-than-men-at-disguising-autism-symptoms

Chapter 7

ADHD Aware (2021) *ADHD Symptoms.* Brighton, UK: ADHD
Aware. Accessed on 19/05/2022 at https://adhdaware.org.uk/
what-is-adhd/adhd-symptoms

Dodson, W. (2022) *How ADHD Ignites Rejection Sensitive*

Dysphoria. ADDitude Magazine. Accessed on 16/05/2o22 at www.additudemag.com/rejection-sensitive-dysphoria-and-adhd

Wilkinson, L.A. (n.d.) *Alexithymia, Empathy, and Autism*. Wetherby, UK: Living Autism. Accessed on 19/05/2o22 at https://livingautism.com/alexithymia-empathy-autism

Chapter 8

The Yale Center for Dyslexia and Creativity (2o17) *Richard Rogers, Architect*. New Haven, CT: Yale. Accessed on 19/05/2o22 at https://dyslexia.yale.edu/story/richard-rogers

INDEX

A

ACAS 14
Ackroyd, Dan 38
adaptations
    for ADHD 43–4
    for autism 38–9
    for communication 80
    for dyslexia 32
    for dyspraxia 47
    for emotions 96–7
    for processing 61
    for unwritten rules 88–9
    for working memory 68
ADHD
    adaptations for 43–4
    celebrities with 42, 43
    description of 40–2
    emotions 90, 94–6
    experience of 39–40
    and hyper-focus 42–3
    key takeaways 49
    prevalence of 40
    and processing 55, 60
    reflection points 50
ADHD Aware 90
ADHD UK 40
Adjust training company 11–12
Adult Side of Dyslexia, The
    (Sandman-Hurley) 29
Archer, D. 42
autism
    adaptations for 38–9
    barriers for 32–3
    celebrities with 38
    communication 71–2, 74–5, 76–7
    diagnosis of 35–6
    emotions 90, 92
    in employment 12, 32, 72
    key takeaways 48–9

language used for 33–5
masking 85–8
misconceptions about 36–7
myths about 36–7
problem-solving 101
and processing 52, 57–8, 60
prevalence of 35
reflection points 50
stereotypes about 37
and unwritten rules 82, 84, 85–8

B

Barnfield, K. 38
Battersby, K. 38
BBC News 58
BBC Newsround 88
BBC Yorkshire 44
Bedigan, M. 43
Biles, Simone 42
Blume, Harvey 16
Branson, Richard 30
Bremner, Rory 43
British Dyslexia Association 28

C

Castellon, Siena 57–8, 85
CDC 36
communication
    adaptations for 80
    different styles of 75–7
    difficulties with 70–5
    in education 79
    in employment 77–9
    key takeaways 80–1
    reflection points 81
Crompton, C.J. 33

D

Deschanel, Zooey 43
diagnosis of neurodiversity 26–7
diversity in neurodiversity 19–23
Dodson, W. 93
double empathy problem 33
Dutton, J. 41
dyslexia
    adaptations for 32
    celebrities with 30
    in education 28–30
    key takeaways 47–8
    misconceptions about 28–9
    overlapping diagnoses 28
    problem-solving 103–4
    and processing 52
    reflection points 49–50
    stigma 29
dyspraxia
    adaptations for 47
    celebrities with 45–6
    coordination 44–5
    key takeaways 49
    planning and organisation 45
    prevalence of 44
    reflection points 50
Dyspraxia Association 44

E

education
    communication in 79
    and dyslexia 28–30
Elizabeth, D. 74
emotional difference 94–5
emotional regulation 92–3

emotions
  adaptations for 96–7
  emotional difference
    acceptance 94–5
  emotional regulation 92–3
  difficulties with 90–2
  key takeaways 97
  managing feelings of
    difference 93–4
  reflection points 98
employment
  communication in 77–9
  and neurodivergent skills 22
  people with autism 12, 32, 72
  problem-solving 101–2
Evans-Williams, C.V.M. 33
Evening Standard 46

F

Farrington, C.P. 33
Freeth, B. 43

G

Gannon, L. 38
GCHQ 22, 101–2
Genge, Ellis 46
Goldberg, Whoopi 30

H

Hannah, Daryl 38
heightened sensory sensitivity 58–60
Higashida, Naoki 71
Holland, K. 46
Honoré, Carl 54
Hopkins, Anthony 38
Hull, L. 35

J

Jordan, Michael 42

K

key takeaways
  ADHD 49
  autism 48–9
  communication 80–1
  dyslexia 47–8
  dyspraxia 49
  emotions 97
  neurodiversity 47
  problem-solving 104
  processing 61–2
  unwritten rules 89
  working memory 68–9

L

Levine, N. 40
Look Me in the Eye (Robinson) 27
Loomes, R. 35

M

Magidoff, S. 54
Malone, Jo 30, 58, 59
Mandy, W. 35
masking 85–8
Mayo Clinic 87
McGuinness, Christine 38
Mead, A. 46
Mel B 43
memory *see* working memory
Miah, Shofa 21
Miller, E. 33
Milton, Damien 33

misunderstandings of
  unwritten rules 84–5
Musk, Elon 37

N

National Autistic Society
  (NAS) 13, 26, 35, 36, 52, 71
neurodiversity
  diagnosis of 26–7
  diversity in 19–23
  individuality in 27
  key takeaways 47
  nurturing 17, 19
  prevalence of 14
  resources for 109–11
*NeuroDiversity: The Birth
  of an Idea* (Singer) 16
neurotypes
  ADHD 39–44
  autism 32–9
  dyslexia 28–32
  dyspraxia 44–7
nurturing neurodiversity 17, 19

O

Office for National
  Statistics (ONS) 12, 72
Ojomu, N. 43
oppositional defiant
  disorder (ODD) 87
overlapping diagnoses
  and dyslexia 28
  and neurodiversity 26

P

Packham, Chris 38

Pang, Camilla 37
Phelps, Michael 41–2
Ploszajski, A. 85
problem-solving
  celebration of 101–4
  in employment 101–2
  eye for detail 102–3
  key takeaways 104
  reflection points 105
  seeing big picture 103–4
processing
  adaptations for 61
  heightened sensory
    sensitivity 58–60
  key takeaways 61–2
  and neurodivergence 51
  reflection points 62
  reflective processing 52–4
  sensory processing 55, 57–61
  sensory seeking 60–1
  super-fast processing 55

R

Radcliffe, Daniel 45–6
reflection points
  ADHD 50
  autism 50
  communication 81
  dyslexia 49–50
  dyspraxia 50
  emotions 98
  problem-solving 105
  processing 62
  unwritten rules 89
  working memory 69
reflective processing 52–4
Robinson, John Elder 27
Rodden, J. 42

Rogers, Richard 104
Ropar, D. 33
Roper, Maxine Frances 54, 65, 67, 96

S

Sandman-Hurley, Kelli 29
sensory processing 55, 57–61
sensory seeking 60–1
Shah, Bev 16
Singer, Judy 16
Spectrum Girl's Survival Guide,
  The (Castellon) 57–8
super-fast processing 55

T

Taylor, B. 33
Thunberg, Greta 74–5, 88
Timberlake, Justin 43
Tobin, A.M. 46

U

unwritten rules
  adaptations for 88–9
  difficulties with 82, 84
  key takeaways 89
  masking 85–8
  misunderstandings 84–5
  reflection points 89

W

Weintraub, S. 43
Welch, Florence 46
Wilkinson, L.A. 92
Willingham, E. 38
working memory
  adaptations for 68
  difficulties with 63–7
  key takeaways 68–9
  reflection points 69

Y

Yale Center for Dyslexia
  and Creativity 104